Cursive Writing

Practice Book

Flash Kids™

A Division of Barnes & Noble Publishing

W9-BRY-851

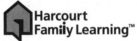
**Harcourt
Family Learning**™

© 2004 by Flash Kids
Adapted from *Write-On, Wipe-Off Handwriting: Cursive* by M.C. Hall
© 2001 by Harcourt Achieve Inc.
Licensed under special arrangement with Harcourt Achieve Inc.

ISBN: 978-1-4114-0086-3

Please submit all inquiries to FlashKids@bn.com

Manufactured in Canada

Lot #:
34 36 38 39 37 35 33
09/15

Flash Kids
A Division of Barnes & Noble
122 Fifth Avenue
New York, NY 10011

Dear Parent,

Even in the age of computers, good cursive handwriting is a must. This book provides an easy and enjoyable way for your child to learn to write cursive letters. More than 100 practice pages provide ample opportunity for your child to master the cursive alphabet and begin writing words and sentences. The fun animal facts and vivid illustrations throughout the book will hold your child's interest as he or she develops these new skills.

Each letter of the alphabet is presented on four pages. Your child will learn how to form each letter, and then practice the letter several times before moving on to words and sentences.

To help your child get the most from this book, follow these simple teaching tips:

- Before your child begins a new letter, demonstrate how to write it on a large piece of paper. Show your child how to make each stroke.

- Have your child trace the letter in the air with his or her index finger.

- Remind your child to use the directional arrows as cues for where to begin each part of the letter.

- Remember that practice makes perfect. Encourage your child to write each letter until he or she feels comfortable.

For added value, the pictures and facts in this book can be used to extend your child's learning. Consider some of these activities:.

- Many of the animals featured in the book are unusual and may be new to your child. Suggest that your child learn more about any animal that seems particularly interesting. Encourage your child to research on the Internet or in a library, and then share the facts with you.

- Invite your child to write and illustrate funny alliterative sentences for each letter. For example, the letter s could be used many times, like in the following sentence: *Six silly snakes sat still on six soft sofas.*

- Print out sentences for your child and ask him or her to "translate" the words into cursive.

- Use the pages at the end of the book to help your child write stories and paragraphs. Be sure to read and offer praise for your child's efforts!

a *a*

a *a*

a *a*

a

a

ant

aphid

ape

Wild Stuff!

The anteater has a long, sticky tongue. It's handy for reaching into an ant or termite nest and grabbing dinner!

A is for anteater.

Anteaters eat ants.

a *a*

a *a*

a *a*

anteater

anteater

Now write your own sentences.

Bb

B B
b b

B

b

baboon

bull

rabbit

Wild Stuff!

The tufts of fur in a bobcat's ears aren't just funny looking. They help the animal hear better.

8

B is for bobcat.

Bobcats are very fierce.

B b

B B

b b

B b

bobcat

bobcat

Now write your own sentences.

C c

C c

c c

C

c

cricket

cobra

raccoon

Wild Stuff !

Crocodiles look scary, but they are good mothers! They guard their nests and take care of their babies.

12

C is for crocodile.

Crocodiles are reptiles.

C c

C   C

c   c

C c

crocodile

crocodile

Now write your own sentences.

Dd

D D D

d d

🍃 Practice Time!

D

d

dolphin

dogfish

adder

Wild Stuff !

Dragonflies haven't changed much since dinosaur times, except in size. Millions of years ago, they had wings three feet wide!

D is for dragonfly.

Dragonflies like ponds.

Dd

D D D

d d d

D d

dragonfly

dragonfly

Now write your own sentences.

E e

E e

e e

E

e

emu

elk

deer

Wild Stuff !

American eels travel back and forth from fresh water to the ocean. Sometimes they wiggle over land to get places!

20

E is for eel.

Eels are long fish.

Ee

E E

e e

E e

eel

eel

Now write your own sentences.

Ff

F

f

fog

wolf

buffalo

Wild Stuff!

The tiny water plants and animals that a flamingo eats are full of things that turn the bird's feathers pink. The more it eats, the pinker it gets!

24

F is for Flamingo.

Flamingos eat fish.

Ff

F

f

Ff

flamingo

flamingo

Now write your own sentences.

G g

$\mathcal{G}$ $\mathcal{G}$

g g

$\mathcal{G}$

g

giraffe

gecko

badger

Wild Stuff !

Gorillas often
use small branches
and leaves to make
beds in trees.

G is for gorilla.

Gorillas are large.

G g

G

g

g g

gorilla

gorilla

Now write your own sentences.

31

Hh

H h

H h

H

h

heron

hornet

cheetah

Wild Stuff!

When danger is near, the hedgehog curls up in a ball of prickly spines!

H is for hedgehog.

Hedgehogs have spines.

Hh

H

h

Hh

hedgehog

hedgehog

Now write your own sentences.

$\mathcal{L}$ $\mathcal{L}$

i i

$\mathcal{L}$

i

itis

iguana

cricket

Wild Stuff!

An impala can jump across a thirty-foot stream in one leap!

36

I is for impala.

Impalas jump high.

$\mathcal{L}\,i$

$\mathcal{L}\quad\mathcal{L}$

$i\quad i$

$\mathcal{L}\,i$

impala

impala

Now write your own sentences.

Jj

J J

j j

J

j

jaguar

jackal

jelly

Wild Stuff!

A jellyfish catches
fish by stinging
them. Some jellyfish
stings can hurt or
even kill people!

J is for jellyfish.

Jellyfish can sting.

$\mathcal{J}\,j$

$\mathcal{J}$

j

jellyfish

jellyfish

Now write your own sentences.

K k

K K

k k

k

k

kiwi

koala

okapi

Wild Stuff

The kookaburra's
call (KOO ka burr uh)
is like a loud laugh.
It is often used in
sound tracks for
jungle movies!

K is for kookaburra.

Kookaburras eat fish.

K k

K K

k k

K k

kookaburra

kookaburra

L is for lemur.

Lemurs can leap.

49

L l

L L

l l

L l

lemur

lemur

Now write your own sentences.

M m

m m
m m

m

m

muskrat

mouse

marmot

Wild Stuff !

The mongoose is
a brave fighter.
It even attacks
and kills poisonous
snakes!

52

M is for mongoose.

Mongooses eat mice.

53

$\mathcal{M}\,m$

$\mathcal{M}\,m$

$m\,m$

$\mathcal{M}\,m$

mongoose

mongoose

Now write your own sentences.

n m

n n

m m

n

n

narwhal

minnow

falcon

N is for needlefish.

Needlefish are narrow.

Wild Stuff!

A needlefish can leap from the water like a flying fish. It can reach a speed of nearly 40 miles per hour!

Nm

n n n

n n

n n

needlefish

needlefish

Now write your own sentences.

O *o*

Practice Time!

o

o

otter

ostrich

moose

An octopus's eight legs have thousands of suckers for holding onto things!

O is for octopus.

Octopuses change color.

O o

O

o

O

octopus

octopus

Now write your own sentences.

P p

P P

p p

p

p

pelican

panda

antelope

Wild Stuff !

An adult platypus
(PLA ti puss) has no
teeth. It uses hard
plates in its bill to
grind up its food.

64

P is for platypus.

Platypuses lay eggs.

P p

P P

p p

P p

platypus

platypus

Now write your own sentences.

Q q

Q

q

Q

q

quail

queen bee

macaque

Wild Stuff!

The quetzal's
(ket SAL) tail feathers
can be more than two
feet long. Sometimes
the bird has trouble
getting its whole
tail into its nest!

Q is for quetzal!

Quetzals are colorful.

69

Q q

Q Q

q q

Q q

quetzal

quetzal

Now write your own sentences.

R r

R R

r r

R

r

reindeer

raccoon

zebra

Wild Stuff!

The rhinoceros is the largest living land animal besides the elephant!

R is for rhinoceros.

Rhinos have horns.

73

R r

R R

r r

R r

rhinoceros

rhinoceros

Now write your own sentences.

$\mathscr{S}s$

$\mathscr{S}$ $\mathscr{S}$

s s

$\mathscr{S}$

s

skunk

starfish

opossum

Wild Stuff !

The sloth spends most of its life hanging upside down in trees. It can take a whole day for a sloth to move from one tree to another!

76

S is for sloth.

Sloths are very slow.

77

$\mathcal{S}s$

$\mathcal{S}$

s

$\mathcal{S}$

sloth

sloth

Now write your own sentences.

$\mathcal{T}t$

$\mathcal{T}$ $\mathcal{T}$
t t

$\mathcal{T}$

t

toucan

tortoise

otter

Wild Stuff!

Turtles have been around since before the time of the dinosaurs. That's more than 200 million years!

T is for turtle.

Turtles are reptiles.

$\mathcal{It}$

More Practice Time!

$\mathcal{I}$ $\mathcal{I}$

t t

$\mathcal{I}t$

turtle

turtle

Now write your own sentences.

Uu

U u

u u

u

u

urial

skunk

tuna

Wild Stuff !

Baby sea urchins aren't much like their parents. They look like upside-down umbrellas!

U is for urchin.

Urchins live in water.

$\mathcal{U}\,u$

$u\quad u$

$u\quad u$

$u\quad u$

urchin

urchin

Now write your own sentences.

$\mathcal{V}v$

V V

w w

🍂 Practice Time!

V

w

arizona

vote

beaver

88

V is for vulture.

Vultures are buzzards.

$\mathcal{V}\ \mathcal{u}$

$\mathcal{V}\ \mathcal{V}$

$\mathcal{u}\ \mathcal{u}$

$\mathcal{V}\ \mathcal{u}$

vulture

vulture

Now write your own sentences.

Ww

W W
w w

W

w

warthog

whale

owl

Wild Stuff!

A walrus can weigh as much as two tons! It uses its large tusks to dig for food on the ocean floor.

92

W is for walrus.

Walruses can swim.

Ww

W W

w w

W w

walrus

walrus

Now write your own sentences.

$\mathcal{X}x$

X

x

X

x

Xx

Xx

lynx

Wild Stuff!

Xenopus
(ZEEN uh puss)
is the scientific name
of the African frog.
Xenopus tadpoles have
see-through skin!

96

X is for xenopus.

A xenopus is a frog.

$\mathcal{X} \, x$

x x

x x

$\mathcal{X} \, x$

xenopus

xenopus

Now write your own sentences.

Yy

Y Y

y y

Y

y

yak

monkey

coyote

Wild Stuff!

Yellow jackets make paper nests out of plant matter and saliva. They eat insects and spiders.

100

Y is for yellow jacket.

Yellow jackets sting.

Yy

Y Y

y y

yellow jacket

yellow jacket

Now write your own sentences.

Zz

Z

z

zebra

grizzly

gaggle

Wild Stuff !

The zebu (ZEE boo) is a strange-looking cow. It has a hump on its back and big, droopy ears!

104

Z is for zebu.

Zebus are white cows.

105

Z Z

z z

z z

z z

zebu

zebu

Now write your own sentences.

Practice.

A a   B b

C c   D d

E e   F f

G g   H h

I i   J j

K k   L l

M m   N n

O o   P p

Q q   R r

S s   T t

U u   V v

W w   X x

Y y   Z z

Finish each sentence.

My favorite animal

is

because

It lives in

It eats

Draw your animal.

Write the animal's name beneath each picture.

_____

- -

_____

_____

- -

_____

_____

- -

_____

_____

- -

_____

_____

- -

_____

_____

- -

_____

_____

- -

_____

_____

- -

_____

Writing Time!

- Tell about your own pets.

- Pretend you are a wild animal.
  Write a letter to humans.

- Make a list of endangered animals.

- Explain how people should treat wild animals.

- List twenty animals you have seen.